Written by Wendy Macdonald
Illustrated by Jenny Mountstephen

Contents

Harcourt Achieve
Rigby • Saxon • Steck-Vaughn

www.HarcourtAchieve.com
1.800.531.5015

The School in the Sky

With these characters . . .

"You have risked

Setting the scene . . .

Ang and her family live in a village high in the Himalayas. Norbu, her older brother, goes to find work in the city.

Ang wants to write to Norbu, but no one in Sondup can read or write.

When the villagers help an explorer in the mountains, it leads to an unexpected development in Sondup.

your life for me . . ."

CHAPTER 1

"Are you going on a journey, Norbu?" Ang asked her brother. He was sewing new leather soles onto his felt boots.

"I am going to the city to find work, little sister," he answered.

"Is the city far away?" Ang asked.

"Oh, it is a long way," said Norbu. "It is seventeen days' walk just to get there."

When the boots were finished, Norbu rolled up his warmest blanket, took some food, and said good-bye to the family. They were all sad to see him go, for they knew he would be away a long time.

He strode off down the narrow, twisting path that led away from the village and down into the valleys.

Ang waved until he was out of sight.

Ang's village was called Sondup and it was high up in the Himalayan mountains, the highest mountains in the world.

Sondup was only a small village of a few houses. Everyone there had to work hard, growing barley and looking after sheep and goats.

Ang's father carried loads from village to village, in a big wicker basket strapped to his back. It was hard work and he was often tired.

One day when Norbu had been gone a long time, Ang asked her mother, "Where is Norbu?"

Her mother looked worried. "I don't know," she said. "He must have reached the city by now. I hope he is alright."

"How can we find out where he is?" said Ang.

"Perhaps the shepherds will know," her mother suggested. So Ang asked a shepherd from the next village.

"Do you know where my brother is? I want to know if he is well and if he has found work."

The shepherd shook his head. "I will ask the other shepherds," he replied, "perhaps they have heard." But no one knew anything about Norbu. Then the shepherd said, "If you write your brother a letter, I will see that it gets to the city."

"That's a good idea," said Ang, and she ran off home to find her mother.

"Mother," she said, "why don't we write Norbu a letter?"

"How can we do that?" said her mother. "I cannot write."

So that night Ang asked her father. "Father," said Ang, "why don't we write a letter to Norbu and find out how he is?"

Her father smiled at her. "That's a very good idea," he said, " but I can't write."

"If no one here can write, we can never send Norbu a letter," said Ang sadly.

Her father looked thoughtful. "If we had a school in this village, all the children could learn to read and write," he said.

"Maybe some parents could learn, too," suggested Ang's mother. "But a school costs a lot of money. We could never afford such a thing."

CHAPTER 2

Then one day a famous explorer came to Sondup. He had come to climb the mountains.

In the village he hired men to help him carry his equipment. They carried his tents and food and oxygen up the mountain so that he would be able to climb right to the top.

Ang's father and the other men of the village were strong and were good climbers. They carried the explorer's stores far up the mountain. When all the stores had been put in place the men returned to the village. The explorer and his team camped on the mountain ready to begin their climb.

Three days later a man came hurrying down to the village. He brought news that the explorer had been badly hurt.

He had fallen into a crevasse in the ice and had broken his arm. He had had to spend a night in the bitter cold of the mountain without shelter.

Now he was very sick, and his hands and feet had frostbite. If he was not brought down from the mountain he would die.

Ang's father and another man set out to rescue the explorer. A fierce wind was blowing and the two men saw an avalanche high above them. They slipped and slid but at last they found the injured man. He could not walk so

they tied him to a stretcher and carried him down the mountain.

In some places they had to lower the explorer down on a rope. It was perilous work, but at last they reached the village safely.

The explorer was very grateful to the men who had saved him. "You have risked your life for me," he said. "If it were not for your bravery I would be dead. What can I do for you in return?"

"We would like a school for the children in our village," said Ang's father, "so they can learn to read and write."

"That would be a very good thing," said the explorer. "I will try to help."

CHAPTER 3

When he was better, the explorer went back to his own country, but he did not forget his promise.

Months went by. It was winter in the Himalayas. There were not many travelers on the mountain but Ang asked each one: "Have you heard anything about Norbu?" But no one had.

Then, one day in the spring, Ang saw a man coming up the path to the village with a big sheet of corrugated iron on his back. "What is that for?" she asked him.

"Aha," said the man, "you'll find out," and he winked at her and went away. Then more men came, with more iron. Some carried hammers, nails, and wood, and others had big coils of wire rope. Last of all came a man with a rolled up piece of paper under his arm.

"Are you a teacher?" asked Ang.

The man smiled. "No, I'm the foreman," he said. Then he unrolled his plans and said, "Now, let's get to work."

CHAPTER 4

First the villagers made a level piece of ground. Then they dug the foundation and made stone walls.

They put the sheets of iron on top to make the roof. Then they made doors and windows and benches and chairs.

Lastly they put heavy stones on the roof and tied them down with wire rope so that the winter gales would not blow the iron away.

They had made a school.

"Now the children in this village can learn to read and write," said Ang's father.

"Can I go to the new school?" asked Ang.

"You will be the first," nodded her father.

"But a school is no use without a teacher," said Ang. "And we don't have one."

"A teacher is coming," she was told.

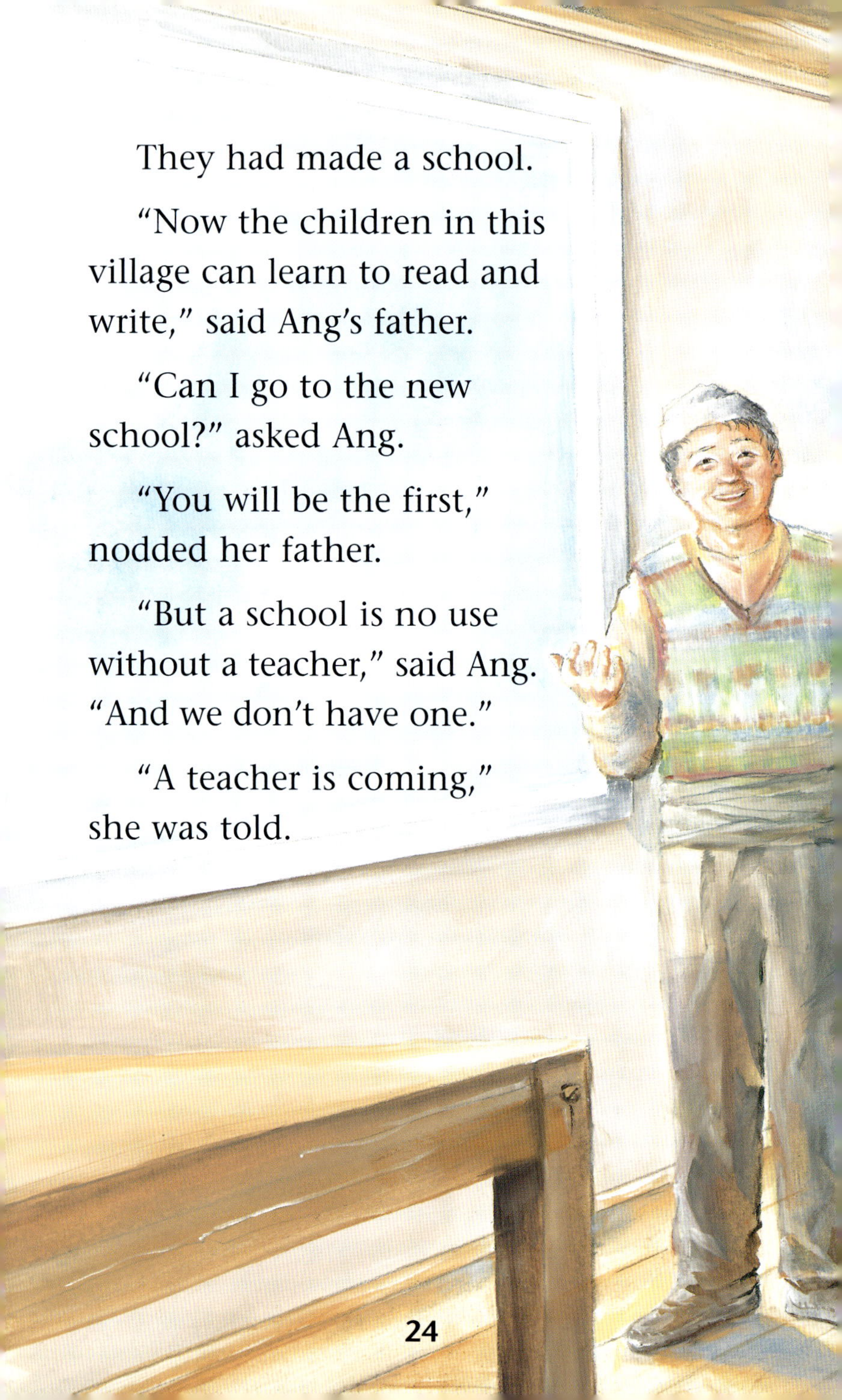

When the school building was finished the villagers had a party. The explorer and his friends came. People from the city came and took photos of the new school. Everyone sang and danced. Only Ang was worried.

"Where is the teacher for our school?" she asked. Everyone said, "Do not worry. A teacher is on the way." But still no teacher came.

Ang began to think that she would *never* be able to write Norbu a letter.

CHAPTER 5

But far away in the city, Norbu was shown the photos in the newspapers. "Look at this: a school in my village! How my little sister Ang has grown."

"I knew you were from Sondup," said Norbu's friend. "You must go as a guide with the new teacher. She is afraid she will get lost in the mountains."

"She is right," said Norbu. "It is easy to get lost. I will see that she gets there safely."

So one day two figures were seen trudging up the path to Sondup. When Ang saw them she jumped up and down for joy.

"Norbu! Norbu!" she called out. "You have come back."

"Yes, little sister," said Norbu and he hugged her.

"What have you got on your back?" she asked.

"I have brought you presents from the city," said Norbu. "I have a new teakettle for our mother, a pair of new shoes for our father, and a book of colored pictures for you. And I have brought something better than all these things. Here is Pema, the teacher for your new school."

The whole village crowded round to welcome Norbu and the new teacher.

"Now we have a school and a teacher," said Ang's father. "The children will soon be able to read and write."

"Yes," said Ang, "and we have found Norbu, too."

"Mountain Guide"

When Norbu left his village high
It made his little sister cry.
"A school," she said, "would make me better.
I could write Norbu a letter."

So they built a school but no teacher came
For the path was steep over rough terrain.
Till Norbu said, "I will be her guide,"
And he brought her safe up the mountainside.